MW01539654

ASH STEPS

M. TRAVIS LANE
ASH STEPS

POEMS

Cormorant Books

Copyright © 2012 M. Travis Lane
This edition copyright © 2012 Cormorant Books Inc.
This is a first edition.

No part of this publication may be reproduced, stored in a retrieval system or
transmitted, in any form or by any means, without the prior written consent of the publisher or a
licence from The Canadian Copyright Licensing Agency
(Access Copyright). For an Access Copyright licence,
visit www.accesscopyright.ca or call toll free 1.800.893.5777.

Canada Council   Conseil des Arts   ONTARIO ARTS COUNCIL
for the Arts   du Canada   CONSEIL DES ARTS DE L'ONTARIO

Canadian   Patrimoine   Canadä
Heritage   canadien

The publisher gratefully acknowledges the support of the Canada Council for the Arts and the
Ontario Arts Council for its publishing program. We acknowledge the
financial support of the Government of Canada through the Canada Book Fund (CBF) for our
publishing activities, and the Government of Ontario through the Ontario Media Development
Corporation, an agency of the Ontario Ministry of Culture,
and the Ontario Book Publishing Tax Credit Program.

LIBRARY AND ARCHIVES CANADA CATALOGUING IN PUBLICATION

Lane, M. Travis (Millicent Travis), 1934–
Ash steps / M. Travis Lane.

Poems.
ISBN 978-1-77086-096-4

I. Title.

PS8573.A55A88 2012   C811'.54   C2012-900281-X

Cover art and design: Angel Guerra/Archetype
Interior text design: Tannice Goddard, Soul Oasis Networking
Printer: Sunville

Printed and bound in Canada.

MIX
Paper from
responsible sources
FSC
www.fsc.org   FSC® C014078

CORMORANT BOOKS INC.
390 Steelcase Road East, Markham, Ontario, L3R 1G2
www.cormorantbooks.com

For my friends who have encouraged,
supported, and read my poems

CONTENTS

The Tenant

Stone Dusk

A Firefly's Pentecost

The Tenant

THE CONFLUENCE

A milky brown, the rivers slid
below the greying cottonwoods
like great pale snakes. I found them dull.
The bridge from which I looked at them
seemed nothing much. A beggar
wished me blessings just half way.
Early, I thought, and chilly.

To sit all morning on this arc
of concrete! That man seemed
like the small bubble balancing
midway in a plumber's level,
calm as the waters seemed to be,
bland, muscular, indifferent.

On the other side the written past
stirred mildly in the grasses,
not quite washed over, settled. The carved stones
seemed wrong. I wanted wood, ephemera,
feathers and cloth. I wanted leaves
that as I watched them faded brown
and then into the silky grey
of water, weather, passing time.

Light flickered as if the rivers stirred
the shadows, clouds, the sanded paths.
Nothing seemed solid, nothing sealed,

not even the graveyard markers or
the new church growing within the old
like a sapling on a felled nurse log.
Nothing was settled, not history,
nor the rainbow bridge on which
a beggar sat like a balancing.
Whoever passed he blessed.

THE HILL CEMETERY AT ST. MARTIN'S

A good view out to sea, it was, but now
close-wooded, not even the weather shows,
but only the eastern lookout, blank,
grey, mostly, sometimes greeny blue,
and the wool clouds lowering slowly like a blind.
(Nor can you put out lookout lights, you being dead,)

A cleared hill, once, the highest round about,
but now all bush: birch, poplar, crab, spruce, alder,
fir — the straggly trees that rise up from your spines
as if you were not nutrient enough. But someone could
have kept these junk trees cleared away.

There's a small white fence
around one grave; a tree
thrusts up within it as if it,
the tree, were what the fence was for.

The ones who buried you up here are dead,
and tucked away down valley in grassed lots.
You, with your long view now obscured,
what would you once have thought of this?

Yet someone comes, rememberers, though not of you.
The ones who want to keep the woods.
Have the woods gone back to what they were?
Unlikely, you did so much lumbering!
And the river — oh that would grieve you so —

is barren, not like the salmon-clogged
fierce water that it was — and ships?
I do not see them, now, out there.

As for the folk that were here before,
the earlier ones — we have to imagine them,
their long, dark, spruce-thatched bungalows.
You are dissolving into them,
just ghosts after all. The rememberers
care for the trees, the cliffs, the grass,
even the river, which runs so low.
All these, and even the sea, may change.

We hang on as we can, dear hearts.
But not much lasts.

THE SEA BEYOND THE CHURCH

The church stands near the sea on the great marsh flats
where winds assault its twinned wood towers
as if their salt hands were hard light,
empty as dry reeds, flutes, or pipes.

The bitter weather scours the fields,
salt meadows where the low barns slouch,
in which the harrows, rakes, hung up
seem to be up forever, now,
and the boats, in their shabby tarpaulins,
rot on their racks.

The sea beyond the church is bare,
neither the fish nor the pentecost
left for us, impenitents
who don't know how to pray.
We took too much too carelessly, forgot
even at mass forgot,
the pale world rubbing at the rim
of our myopic dreams.

ASH STEPS

i
No frog
jumped into the water bin.
But something fell, and for a while
that tepid mirror shifted, squirmed,
and shook beige shreds of floating leaf,
a pigeon feather, dust,
larvae perhaps.

ii
The ash steps wet with dew,
a toenail paring of the moon:
means rain. I think of you
white-ankled through the gauze
mosquito net we salvaged for our bed
in this tin/cardboard/canvas town
that, mountainous,
shadows the city where you work.
It`s late. You will not come.

iii
The willows moult; the grasses brown.
Fog silts the river. I write you from
this frontier post which is
like all frontiers these days, long past.

What are the soldiers watching for?
If you came to me by the longest road
there is, I'd go out, still, to look for you,
even as far as yesterday. That far.

iv

Late, and the reeds were pewter.
Marsh birds slept.
The aspens by the boardwalk creaked.
The highway plashed its spinning lights
across dark water.
"Closed! You shouldn't be walking here!"
Moon, also, without privilege.

v

One light, one flickering tv,
faces like fish in aquariums,
a plastic bucket, drinking cups,
brochures, hair dryer,
an ironing board,
a clock, and a triple pillowed bed:
a room infected with loneliness.

vi

"Look out for the seals," she said. "When the tide is right
they come up toward the paving for the scraps."
I never saw them, though I looked.
The tide was tufted with dusty foam
(which cannot have been good for them.)

On the outside porch of the hotel,
little girls
in heels, black strapless minis, and a bride
all legs and long goose-pimpled arms.
No seals.
We settled to our napkins and cold rolls.

vii

The river is clouded like mutton jade, ice
trampled, bruised, and fragmented.
The streetlights in their pumpkin orange
a sort of constant Halloween.

By the high school there's
a scoured first-base, white-sanded,
round, and glinting as the cars'
long headlights, turning, cross the field.

Tonight has the sort of loneliness
I'd take for yours, but now,
I want some sort of
steadfast and sororal beacon

like a moon's, perhaps,
which might say "It's not yet too late,"
or, better, "You're soon home."

viii

Hearing the Lights at Yoho,
or feeling them, a prickle of pale green
as, sometimes, after a coyote's howl
the pale down of your forearm stirs.

Welcoming, sometimes, the wilderness —
and the fire logs, stacked within.

ix

The Narrows is black. The sea
might still be glistening
below these sombre cliff-tops, but
the harbour, valley, the steep streets
are spangled like a milky way
of tiny, glittering solitudes,
under the Rock's austere gaze.

Someone's awake. Perhaps more than one.

IN A GLASS DARKLY

It's night, and where we sit
together, watching the failing fire
sink and grow red,
the windows shine
with our dim selves reflected, and, beyond
those darkened shapes,
a nightscape of strange things
not clear, and not familiar —
though nothing's changed,
except what changes all the time.

We can't see out
if the kitchen light,
bedazzling from the ceiling,
clouds the glass
with its peculiar mirror of our selves,
and yet we want that glass
between ourselves and the outdoors.

Whatever it is that courses through
our yards and gardens, midnights
on these crisp winter evenings leaves no mark
on the glassed snow.
What is out there?
Turn out the house lights and we see
only the lights of midnight: stars,
moon, clouds refracting earth-lights; they
might let us know
something of darkness.

But not that orange street-light, much too loud,
which severs dusk from twilight and decides
against the stars, against the dark,
a constant semi-noon-light,
full of buzz. It tells us nothing we don't know.

What we see in reflections late at night
in mirrors stretched on darkness or the pale
wave-rippled brilliance of a pond,
are only surfaces which close
against our look.

So Dido saw,
having a dark heart for her thought,
an old flame glimmer,
but the fire
was Carthage, burning,
death, her brilliant past.

OLD PARENT

The moon that seems so far up in the sky
is scarred like an old stomach: stretch-marks,
pox, psoriasis. It hangs
ill and uneven over us,
as if it mirrored us and not our sun.
Look at it fading thinner as our shade,
like a strong hand, eclipses it
and thumbs it into blackness. A thread
gleams at the odd horizon and the moon
pulls out, old parent, and returns
to brood unblinking on our dark.

No longer the unreachable, it looks distressed,
like an abandoned house
whose blackened, empty windows sag,
untenanted, unwelcoming —
a sarsen in an ungrazed field.
We want to tease it into words,
a kind of whiteboard for our script,
but nothing's left for us to say.

Meanwhile, the cities of poetry, of myth,
religion, where we were born,
are killing each other: Nazareth,
Haifa, Beirut, or Teheran:
their borders hangnailed, vaporous.
Dust on the moon or the desert wind.
Write, said the angel. What shall I write?
And where?

THE STEEPLE

A small town set adrift,
a set, a cardboard cut-out, a loose book
whose pages, falling open, fall away.

Water, I guess, wells somewhere, or a brook
tied to the foot of the cottonwood.
In the scratchy rushes a new fawn
falters its early footsteps.

War had not emptied these houses; life
had merely packed up, moved on.
Church, shed, store, barn, a rusting truck
slumped in the ditch like a snake's shed skin.

The telephone still slings its line across the fields.
The steeple, too, enacts its cairn.
Scratching the sky with its fingernails,
it wants to be leaving messages
for those who have left or those now left behind,

or us, two tired travellers whose train
burrows into the afternoon.

EVENING AT THE SMALL HOTEL

Remember the skinny, leaning trees
with bark in blue and coral shags,
and the tiny doves, brown-grey,
that scrabbled in the forecourt's sand?

Beyond us, like a plain of dreams,
broad musky fields, horizon-hemmed
by shadow-mauved, thatched houses,
threads of smoke, dim tufts of heavy oaks and palms,

and halfway there, like a painter's point,
a man, red shirt, machete, going home.
(The evening noisy with insect calls.)

PAST MIDNIGHT, AVIGNON

Plane trees at night: knobbed harlequins
with white, patched leaves.
The lights have turned off in the merry-go-round
so the mute horses cannot dance
nor the Alice teacup spin and spin.

The plaza is dark, except the trees
hold like dark peaches the late street lamps
with their fragrance of moth-wing and cigarettes.
The shutters are up.

Don't talk any more. On the balconies
only the shadows are listening.
Even the cats have gone to bed;
even the moon.

CIRCLING POLARIS

A wood flute, rather badly played.
Small bells.

Four bears, an ape,
all in red fez,
play monkey-in-the-middle.

Claw-click, a barefoot shuffling,
the ape a little nervous —
(castanets)
bangs its tin crackers.

Ursi make their cardinals.
The rose complete,
they drop to fours.
Exeunt.

MASKS

In the museum
the masks were all bad dreams:
a princess white as burned ash,
an orange fire dog, a raven made of spikes,
a lizard with feathers and ancient hair.

The drug store masks you had seen before:
those soft-sided flaccid masks
that mimic the faces of government,
Spiderman, Elvis, the pink-fanged Count.

The face itself is a sort of mask —
(the women at the nursing home
whose faces each day grow more alike:
bone husks, anonymous ivory) —

At the end of the field in a brownish pile
are skulls, not rotting vegetables,
and they are not dreams.

We choose a face as we choose a mask,
painting, designing —
an awkward sort of poetry, but still
a claim.

Shall I be lynx, that sister of spots,
sag-bellied and jewelled,
with a broken tooth,
hunching along the sour ground,

bearing an arrow in my womb
death shall deliver, that carrier —
a letter of sorts?

Or horse, skew-eyed, piebald,
my mane in corn rows,
Christmas bells?
For this is the present, and I can choose.
(As for the past,
it is ivory.)

DALI'S "SANTIAGO"

The horse's penis scares me, with its star
on a mushroom cloud
below a barefoot shouting saint who scrapes
a pallid cross against the sky —

Behind the monstrous leaping horse
an unsupported pillar holds
a sort of roofless raftering
or trellis on the blank blue sky.

On the beach
a girl in a white hijab smirks. The sea,
forgetting tide or wind, is flat
as asphalt, but
the stallion's cloud-figged testicles
insist on their centrality.

Which is divine — that nearly naked man,
or the white stallion's semened fog?
The little human giggles in her shawl.
She is not reverent.

EXTREME EKPHRASIS

We could suppose
that what we like in paintings is ourselves,
or something in us. We respond;
we make ourselves at home in them, or,
sometimes wish we couldn't, but —
whether the work upsets or soothes,
art speaks for us, is us — presents us
as what we present.

Begin at home. That painting of a duck.
But is it duck as duck, or you and I
as duck, and looking awkward, here
under a shabby lotus leaf?
What are we up to, living as we do,
as that duck in particular?
(Our human eyes the one disguise
we can't remove.)

Just paint and line?
A flat plane of false weights?
That hardly seems enough.
A mood at least: insouciance (that duck?)
or even dank and dismal moods
we'd be at home with, telling us
about ourselves what we might know.

Or, this collection of small dots
against a granite background, over which
small flourishes of red, assertions
of plain yellow. "Abstract."
How much it pleases us!

It's not an arrangement that reflects
or poses nothing we can say —
but like beach pebbles we pick up,
continues to be beautiful:
the storage of another world
than ours, and ours because
we picked them up.

The conscious grace of animals
(say horses, cats) composes
their arenas. We, as well,
inscribe our selves upon our space,
interpret. Speech
is our ekphrasis: life
acknowledged, breath by breath.

HORSE

A meadow,
a horse, I think still young —
the wind had changed direction
and blown back again.
It won't come to the fence.

It was wild last night,
such wind!
The meadow is dotted with broken twigs,
cones, the occasional epiphyte —

This morning,
when the rooster crowed,
the callas were thick as our golden glow
against the slanting privies in the mist.

The grass is too long.
The restaurant
won't have our breakfasts ready, and
you, horse, do not know me —

tossing your mane
as skittish as a cat.
I thought perhaps
you were showing off.

Or the wind last night
had left you still afraid. Scary, in fact,
for both of us.
And you so pretty,
your long, colt's legs.

And the fierce little tabby
who minds the motel,
louring beneath a straggling bush
that hasn't yet bloomed!

The wind-shy horse has cantered down the hill.
That was so many years ago,
and I don't speak Horse.
Even my Cat is a foreign tongue,
or a little bit foreign.

Small Pedro did not flee,
but he did not come to my finger tips.

THE CHOIR

Below the dangling mangrove roots
the sea caves suck and draw the tides
to a salt pond where jellyfish
rise toward the sunlight,
sink at dusk.

A pond of moons, blunt bubbleheads,
white tapioca parablooms, pale tutus,
rain in water, or Doré's albed choir in Paradise,
these fish, which sing the simplest hymn.
I am, says each. *I am.*

HUNTINGTON BEACH

The picnic lot, half shaded, with sandy tables,
rusting taps, and a dirty hedge through which a cat
tracking the steps of a grackle slides —
the sea can be heard just barely through the thatch
of cockspur, sea grass, bindweed, on the dune
that hummocks like a glacis for a fort
the Parks have long neglected. Asphalt walks
turn into board; sand covers them.
Someone's transistor bawls away.

We can leave Poppa here in the shade
with a soda can and his book.
He wishes the music would be turned off,
but he'll sleep. The youngsters will go,
eventually, with their green-furred dice
shaking against their windshield's time.
The oak trees drop their litter overhead.
We'll find him with an acorn in his hat,
leaves blown against his elbows.
Pack him up. Let him drive home, but carefully.
He might be sleepy. He'll let us know.

COB'S WEB

The cob's in the far corner of her web,
bright as a dropped earring, jet, or gilt,
almost, she thinks, invisible.
I've seen her, hanging upside down,
in the scrub corner of the house,
shingle and eave her privacy,
and all her silver glitter, woden-home,
a sort of rainbow crossing, bridge,
seemed vacant, uninhabited.

Her glamour is an anagram of fate,
where we, like small daft insects tread
pure silver, the abyss of space,
not seeing where the dragon waits.
She need not snip the thread
that swaddles, seems to pupal us;
we carry it along with us
as if it were a life-line, air-hose,
tether. Where we go — that other world —
shines in her lace, exquisite as wet stars.
We know it's there, sure-footed as we are.

THE TENANT

The house has its own business, below
it, almost never seen, the animal
minds its own affairs, late nights.
Only the footprints in the snow
or, sometimes, just a glimpse predawn
of that effulgent spreading tail,
black, white, a sort of mourning fan,
reminds us
of what lives with us.

Like a grief kept in a cupboard,
where the door, sometimes, unlatches
as the house shifts, or by carelessness —
and there it is, the animal
we hardly ever see,
and do not need to look at to recall.
It's there, part of the house's
business, like breakfast, letters,
gardening, all those day time
excursions. Coming home
the house seems warm, seems welcoming,
and isn't it? Of course.

What's not there's not conspicuous.
The night-time tenant sleeps
under the eiderdown of day,
turned off, enclosed, in silences
below our noisy housekeeping.
It's easy to believe, sometimes,
it is not there.

Stone Dusk

PRELUDE

Here in the milky half light of near dawn
snow folds its separate crystals
as if each flake a flower closed against the rain.
Small rods of silver, the odd fist
of still extended filigree, have stuck to some.

A roof becomes grey marble; lawn
a shorthand scribble. Birds
hunch in the reeds. The muskrat's thatch
she had been fiddling with again
is powdered like a sugared bun. Ponds
glow like glass opals, an oily sheen.

What music for this not yet day
that weather shutters? A whispered rasp from a tin flute?
Or the small insistence of tabla drums
that squat like cats at their player's feet?

The snow becomes more definite:
white, black, and white.

"I WOULD HAVE TOLD YOU"
(John 14:2)

Children alone in the hospitals
watching machines tick time away,
a world of closed doors closing —
each empty day holds emptiness
like a last cup.

At the nursing station stands
an artificial Christmas tree
with loops of caterpillar foil.
Outside the drowsy snowflakes fall.

Does sleep, which comes, at last,
unwanted or desired
bring only another hospital,
grander, perhaps?

Keeper of all things,
keep them now. The screens
that mark their passage, their ebb tides,
malfunction, show us snow.

THIRD STROKE
"… as a little child"

Three times. What he was once
has now been changed. The kindliness,
puréed by a blocked artery,
has vanished; in its stead
all the resentful angriness that reason
and compassion had put down.
The childish rage of a two-year-old
has made this old man dangerous,
who once was loving, wise, and good.

What is he, undermined by age?
As if, the whole cathedral gone,
its green man, primitive, still lurks?
We say that good in God survives,
or madness, like a scar, will fade —

We all of us
have our good angel in us and our bad.
What churns up when our mind is harmed
is not our selves, but instances
long put aside, though always there,
ploughed under by our adult life.
What heart does not exist above
a bloody child? Tiger, lamb, and innocent —
we are the hymn read backward, and
we are the hymn.

WAITING

A stem of cloud curls upward like a sigh,
but you've not sighed. Your face is calm
as, waiting without patience, hope, or thought,
the night-caught passengers whose flights
postponed, postpone again. Nothing is cancelled,
nothing set. You have no plans.

Outside, a black flotilla of wild ducks
drifts on the tide. The day, like a white
curtain on thin rings, encloses us.
I hear you breathing steadily. I could
accept a black-winged angel, or a friend
you had lost, years ago, returned: Vi,
maybe, or your sister Millicent.
You think, sometimes, that I am she.

You don't expect your husband yet. The dreams
that crowd your waking hours come from
your childhood: apple trees, those friendly cows —
etc. Not here. A foreign land.
My life and yours slip overboard
and drown in a pale stupor of mild pain.
But should you struggle back to shore?
You told me once you wished to drown,
to swim out, let the long tide take
you to the ocean's rim. That's what
it's doing now, I think. You float.
You do not swim.

AN OLD MACHINE

The mind goes off. It's an old machine.
We cannot expect to be luckier
than those louche women we sometimes see
in the store-front mirrors,
white-headed, strange.

The mind like the old body wanders off,
is not itself, refuses to come home,
and will not answer when, midnights
we wake, we call it, and it won't
recall, or from our dreams return.

These are bad times. We did not know
 we had so much was wrong, one death
upon another, every day.
In the lean quarters of the night
we watch the minutes trickle by.
Us too? we ask. The clock insists.
Us too.

HOW LONG?

How many dear friends have passed away
ahead of us
as if they bore our standards into dark
while we
hover impatient on a shore
we will not leave
but clutch as if to moorings those
particular daisies, that one star
that, summer nights,
turns up across the garage roof
familiar as a street sign, then moves on!

Full summer now, but heavy mists
rot the wet harvests. You,
banners and trumpets on ahead,
emblazon for us the worst of it.
For some of us have dropped off,
mind first to the ditch
that drags down to the river year by year,
no longer ourselves, not wholly.
Sometimes the dimmed self wakens,
knows: "*That's* who I am!"
then sinks back into strangeness and the dusk.

Oh Death, be quick! When we have done,
unhook us, Death, as if you nipped
from clotheslines every worn-out self
and heaped us in a laundry of pure white.
Let us be snow, be water, then.
Let us die quick!

HAPPINESS: IT HAD BEEN HERE

Happiness: it had been here
just a while ago,
settling among the apple trees.

As if we floated on thistledown,
we walked in the perfume of the day —
and nothing else —

not evening over the reddening hills,
or the droning highways, the night hawks' cries,
shadows like tarnish along the road

with, here and there,
a small house with wood butterflies
like laundry not yet taken in.

But this was dusk, not sadness. By the road
grey creatures lurked, anonymous,
the night would hurtle, trample, kill.
Dawn finds the asphalt streaked with blood.

TEMPORARILY LOST

If you walk out far enough in the woods
the time might come
when there will seem no reason to walk back.

Just here, in the semi-dusk of pine,
you might lie down,
and hear the evenings pearl away, the gnats
changing the seconds. The drift of stars, sun,
rain, the squeaking of small birds,
will seem, as your shoulders grow to soil,
the properest adjustment of your life.

This, this is real, this fractioned tininess,
this resting on the movement of the stars,
this deepening into granite, clay,
or water. Why should bones
erect themselves and prance about
and have, oh god, opinions?

Just to lie down like a shed snake skin
and let the soul (if there is a soul)
ooze from the flesh like steam from a cold spring
that on a warm day turns to smoke
or a stray moth
that flutters over carrion or sips
from flowers, or blown
by an unheard-of arctic wind
traverses oceans, continents —
feels nothing but the coldness of the day —

"I am not me — I am just now
too tired to be me.
Let all that's in me puff away —

I might come back."

HER STORY

Most stories have specific shapes, their endings
(there are several) much the same:
first ending ends in marriage,
the second, marriage ends —
(which might be a beginning).

Then there's death (if it's her story, his).
If death occurs quite early, there's
"what happens next?" (Mr. Arabin?)
Sometimes she only carries on
until the end writes R.I.P.,
and chipmunks crack their knuckles
on her grave.

Of course outside plain story lines,
there's war, and famine, politics,
and illness. These don't tidy up.
When they let you out of hospital or jail,
was that the new beginning, or,
was that the start when they took you in?

Now in the pastel corridors
you wait in a short johnny-gown
while adults carrying teddy bears
or wearing Disney-patterned shirts
talk over you
and someone's CNN TV roars.

Is this your next beginning? Peter Pan's
"the great adventure"? No,

it's only turning out, one at a time,
your theatre's long burning lights.

When you are left alone on stage,
there's nothing going on.

PUSH

Dredged halfway from a dream, you
resurface, laugh:
it's "push" you say — it's "push."
"It hurts," you say, and laugh again,
then breaking through,
as if to ozone, you reply
plain courteous answers to the priest
who soothes himself by praying, or
you try a half-remembered joke —
"They joke too much," you say. "It is all push."

I picture a great rock you shove uphill,
or a long swimmer's journey.
You on your own Olympics strive
for the sole crown or medal: life
is what you aim at. What will come
(is coming, soon I think) is death.

But push! The mountain waits for you
beyond some sort of golden door,
and why should you be lost? Or anyone?
But those far shores are hard to gain —
or that far peak.

It's "push," you say, and grimace, smile,
and push away. Perhaps it's oars.
I should imagine you

the Charon of your boat ride, but
no mountain, river, lunging sea.
One narrow bed.

Your dying's hard. "It hurts,"
you say, you laugh again. "It is all push."

STONE DUSK

Stone dusk — it seems an emptied trough;
a wall of leaves hangs over it.
No breeze, just claustral absences,
incurious, bereft, but pearling
as the shadows slide. Night,
intense with its own business,
shakes loose from its green cabinet
one bird.

DREAM WORLD

Now while the spring wind washes night,
the spirit in the lawn of sleep meanders,
its attention caught by this or that:
a knot or scruple, a concern.

The mad world of our dreams emits
a steady stream of circumstance
to which sleep's infancy responds:
the anchor of a parent, a strong shade, a dear cat lost —

"Oh, there you are!" just a trifle bewildering,
"but weren't you dead?"
The conscious mind flickers, a little.

We could sleep on
in this wild garden where every flower
is nearly Home but never quite familiar:
the hall, the stairs, the path through the small wood
or the frost-heaved, long-neglected yard.

(Did I miss spring? How could I have!)
As if we had been gone too long, and now are dead,
and wandering as ghosts observe
a world we cannot enter.

The harsh wind shaking out of doors
injects its other outer world,
a strangeness nothing yet has touched.
Which room is this I am waking to?

MEN NE CUNNON

The tethering rope is cut.
The boat slips from its narrow berth;
sea gathers it:
the scent of dulse, the saline rust
of voyages.
Above you gulls
cry out in unknown languages.

What hand, what harbour waits for you,
we cannot know.

STUFF

As if holding his death certificate,
he walked around his rooms,
loving for all good reasons every thing
he must put by. He couldn't say "list"
to the living. They would cry.
But this bright yellow ceramic pot,
those tree-and-shadow photographs,
they have stood by his desk for decades!
He wanted to put them in poetry,
a kind of preserve.

"When this you see remember me"
the faded cross-stitch sampler says.
"Remember me!" cried Dido, but
it's only her sadness we recall.
That's what the arts are for, and history:
re-inking names on museum walls.
Never enough. Things are too small.
Like Dorothy's harp-shaped needle case
among the poems at Cornell,
or that plain white dress at Amherst.
Stuff.

Or this cardboard box. It says:
20 Gypsy Queen, 20 Crimson King,
and you carved cat doors on an end and side:
a place for Pocket, to hide in, charge out from, or
sit on, dais, far grander than a couch.
Pocket, who lay across my lap
as stiff as a gladiolus sheaf, diagonal;

who played with such abandon he forgot
his tail was his own, and bit it! Or
how he would terrorize the dog,
then yearn for the dog to sit by him.
He died too young. But don`t we all?
Or piece by piece.

I don't know whose these people are,
or why you kept this on your wall,
now that your desk is empty. Dido cried.
But what I wanted to keep is gone.
Old age is one long funeral. And stuff.
Just lots of stuff.

NOISE

High wind, the hammer of the road,
doors slamming, sirens, telephones,
birds thudding into windows and,
just here, the local church bells, buses, trucks,
the dog translating into dog the weather,
crime reports, the score
of unrelenting politics —

Sleep would be nice if those old tunes
that crank themselves inside my head
would lie down like a tired pet
and curl up into silences.

I want
a night of silence, and no moon
with its sleek, spiffy lustre — rather, fog
that silts among the branches like wet snow.

And now the outdoors has shut up —
even the clanking window chime
two yards up street has lost its tongue.
The fridge, for a moment murmurless,
the furnace relenting, so
I hear the clock-works of my ears,
the frost-cracks as the house shifts,
and your voice.

Always, as I fall asleep, your voice —
I start to hear you say something
I can't quite catch.

CLIMBER

Between a distance and this life,
uphill,
her feet sink in the sand

as if there were no end,
dune, cliff,
this mountain sliding down.

No one
can bring her a ladder,

prisoned
in an hour's glass —

Must climb,
must climb....

I HAVE FORGOTTEN YOUR NAME

I have forgotten your name —
but our husbands were dying together
and our tired nurse was too harsh
(you complained too much, I think she thought)
as if she had not realized
how ill he was —
or as if you had asked
somehow too much —
(inflammation, chapping,
his tenderest parts.)

It was a mixed ward;
very odd.
One chap,
with his large family visiting,
from the reserve,
wanted the curtains around his bed
closed around him and them
in a sort of tent. A privacy.

We didn't mind. The nurses did.
But he had kept on getting up
to "steal" the free food from
the tiny kitchen for the ward.
Sugar perhaps? I didn't know.

We could see from his own family
that they thought him sometimes "difficult" —
(he'd been in a fight) — but that he was
beloved, maybe not
the smartest kid,

but loving, loved —
but was he dying?
I didn't know.

Our husbands were,
though no one said.

He was so young —
kids 5, 8, 10 —
oh, he was young!

But later on
in a different, larger hospital
in the Dying ward,
was a man in his 30's,
and one old man, poor teeth,
and happy, dear fellow, but —
he wanted to go home — and not to any family
but to his tiny room downtown.

He was not sick;
he knew he wasn't,
but used to not knowing what others knew.

And that dear man
who was always alone
whenever I came to sit, play music, read
to my fading husband who
might not ever have heard —
he who brought me his lunch
he could not eat —

Did anyone ever visit him?
That pallid turkey sandwich, that
square milk —
Did he have flowers?
Would he have cared? He did a kindness
for me, for him —

I have a friend
(oh she *is* young)
who had read somewhere
it is healthy to weep
so she goes to sad movies.

She need only wait.
Read the back page of any newspaper
or visit a while in "Palliative."
The tears will come,
and they will be no good to her,
or to anyone.

I WISH THE SNOW WOULD COME DOWN

I wish the snow would come down
softly, as it might but does not
this dry Christmas while I mourn
the Christmases we never had,
or did.

For whom this year is the crèche put up?
For whom the lace-frond scout fir
with its cardboard cutout mermaids,
dragons, cats,
its bells and finger puppets, toys
made and not remembered, now,
by mother, waiting for her death
as if she drifted patient on the tide
she thought once she would swim out on....

I wish the snow would come down and erase
like a soft blessing, not
like that fierce double-handed load
it laid down only yesterday,
a wall, a marble barrier,
impermeable nets of plastic ice —

the traveller, the lover, grandchild, all
sealed, enclosed, undocketed,
without a bed or manger hay
to lie on waiting, hour by hour
while nothing lets up easy, but —

I wish release, the traveller home:
tarmac de-iced, our dense machines
refurbished, cleaned —
I want you, travelling, returned
safe, homely, comfortable, and here —

here, oh I wish you here!
Or that the snow
would come down soft
as an easy sleep — not yet,
perhaps, not yet....

A Firefly's Pentecost

POTLUCK

Some leave the party early;
some too late.
It wasn't a party anyway:
a potluck drawing for short straws.
If one of us
gets left, like Ben Gunn,
dinnerless
while others feast —
the pirates always
lurk off shore.

Sometimes, of course, the shot
runs out.

I've stayed this long.
The great dial spins.
Have I a longer course to run?
Blind Pew delivers his black spot.
"Time's up"
the umpire seems to shout.
"Go home."

GOOD ADVICE

(Mozart's *Drei Knaben*)

The little guys in the balloon
(which is a sort of cotton cloud)
will tell us what we need to know.
Oh, don't despair! They might be birds,
but birds don't need to think of us,
so these are cherubs, angels, boys,
reminders of first principles,
whose bell-like voices jingle in our minds.

They are our childhood's firmament:
the things we always used to know,
and, later, wondered, but they say
"Go on, keep up!" and "Don't despair!"
They are the happy memories
that don't erase, that keep on being there.
"Oh, yes," they say, encouraging,
"Keep on, keep on — and don't despair!"

SHE KEEPS WRITING THE SAME POEM

She keeps writing the same poem,
again, again,
as if it were always raining,
where her mind
bobs at cold anchor near a shore
where it is almost winter,
but not yet.

The black stones roll
and fumble on the beach.
Hail-speckled the sea
sloughs easily its skin,
a snake of pale water.

The rain still rains,
runnels the cliffs,
rubs at the slate silk
of the sound,
fretting, untranquil,
again, again.

THE GHOST

After so long and difficult a trip
I think you might not come to me
but stay there, weary as you are,
on that dark shore.

Merely to watch the water move
might be enough:
the brown reeds threshed by wind,
or the drained mud flats
through which your navigating mind
spelled currents, possibilities.

Now all this shimmers under mist:
a cloudy night, no moon, weak tides.
You might rest a while.
Come up to the house? No, what's the point?
Too much has happened too long ago.
You slip back into water like a mink.

CROWS' BIVOUAC

Crows' bivouac: not a settlement —
a city recomposed in air;
those birches were one night rehung
with black, next morning, bare.

Across the white potato fields
they spread their camp; at the alarm
break up and wheel in air, reconnaissance,
sorties, beyond the barns,

the woods, the half-filled parking lot,
as if to spy alternative redoubts,
or, business left unfinished, or,
a mere refusal to clear out

until their next call rallies them:
Where to? What next?

PRACTICAL MEDITATION

We must be guests in this open world,
welcomed and always welcoming. Alone
we travel and not alone.
No bird inhabits the crystal vaults
all by itself. Our life is a firefly's pentecost,
as splendid in its vanishing
as in its blaze.

Wait for the friend
who leads you in the dark with songs.
Accept the dog, its profane joy,
its greediness.
Give to the moment the moment's needs
but then withdraw.

Shut up the windows, still all noise.
Let the white moth which is your soul
flow where it will, release
your busy mindedness.
An unkind thought may come to you.
Observe it, where it comes from, what it is.
It must not be a stranger.

Let all your thoughts come yammering.
Receive, receive, and recognize. Call each
by name. You are their author, they your clan,
the types of your pathetic dreams, night trolls.
Then let them go. You know them,
need not live with them.

Wait for the friend, the song, the dog.
Epiphanies splash up like waves on windy days
against the green edge of a pier;
you don't have to go out to look for them,
abundant, brief, like fireflies as they are.

WISHING

I wish for forests, meadows, temples of green fields, trees, stars,
a fresh wind setting out. But what I find
is sheds, old tools, outmoded books
no one will ever read again, fire-tidied paths I dare not walk
without a phone, a cane, a whistle for distress —
for should I fall, who'd fetch me out?

And yet the wild calls out to me;
it lurches on the platform of my dreams
and hurtles out beyond me without stop:
the rabbit trails, slant markways in the brush,
torn, yellow traces of full moon,
dry heaves of barren sandhills — nothing I
can follow, catch, climb up on, write.

The stars cry out, a sort of lacy yearning, and
like a last bird at dusk, shall I reply?
I hear, I hear their brilliances.
I clutch my twig.

NEIGHBOUR

(for Marcel Latouche)

That rattling giant, that poplar tree
whose green-sheened branches poked our roof
all winter, and who now
fattens rhubarb coloured buds
like little sucked thumbs —

        the one
whose scruffy, invasive rootlings, cotton-palmed,
broke up our lawn, who walloped the shingles
in heavy winds and shoved and shaded our apple-tree,
and into which each spring I peered,
tracing its pale chartreusy skin
against the darker evergreens —

       is coming down.

On a long ladder like the one
in pictures shinnies to the moon,
our silver bearded neighbour stands
with a small handsaw. So tidily
he drops the branches, day by day,
'til he's been left with a shining pole
which he will whittle and bring down
with ropes, leaving a gap behind
in the western sky.

Will I miss you, old monster?
Perhaps I will. And you'll
(my neighbour has taken care)
miss me.

HOUSE

A well-pathed wood, but rocky further on.
We were here, I think, some years ago,
but now, without you or the dog, much emptier.
Or perhaps I am only going home.
When you think of it,
Dorothy's always going home. And Alice, too,
who runs so hard in one small place
(and all the forest silent, full of names.)

At the forest edge is a hunter's blind,
with Scent Elimination, camera ports.
Might it not serve for a thrifty bear?
What is it I have been looking for
but a home of sorts? But I have a house,
paper, a sort of Wendy house. It follows me
like a dog with nowhere else to go.
I'll wait, it will catch up with me;
it always does.

WINDOW OF LEAVES

leaf translucent, leaf opaque,
leaf shining like green bottle glass,
leaf as dark curtain, window blind:

> among the leaves in the old squirrel nest
> a bird inserts her careful self,
> smoothing her apron, a pillow fluffed —

leaves rock and teeter: pennants flap
as if each long bough held a bird who, striding,
(rearranging) wagged
the whole tree,

or as if breaths
from an unnoted bevy of small winds
(the unreclusive cherubim)
shook out their flags

> the robin stares; her jet eye
> reads the radar of green worlds

below her in my paper chair I scribble notes

GLASS ORPHEUS

Inch high, with a blue sombrero, black
moustache, a chair, and a pale green cello, he's
what's left of a glass trio. The others
shattered long ago. But still this lone survivor plays.
He has an adequate audience:
a jade whale less than half his size,
an even smaller polar bear,
a huge ("life-size") Venetian bee,
and a tiny plastic tiger from
a Christmas cracker Sarah brought.

Musicians want
an audience. Don't poets, too?
That when we sit down seriously
to make of what our best we can —
don't we all want,
present, if only glassily alert,
a charmed, attentive audience?

MONKEY

Cleaning out from under the registers
I found one Lego square,
a pink candle rose for a birthday cake,
and a small plastic monkey, grey as dust.

We had been so well prepared
for all those children who never came:
the bushel basket full of blocks
and vivid, long-tailed dinosaurs,
and the story books.

Shall I send the whole lot down the street
where children I will never know
bury their toys in the play-yard sand?
The heart has its reasons: the monkey stays.
A sort of ghost.

SLEEP DEAR CHILD

Sleep dear child, the night is warm
and you may not be lost.

Let the green curtains of the trees
hang over you, and moss
raise its soft feathers around your head.

No noises now, the wind
won't startle branches into aches,
no bird cry out, the gnats
will flicker out.

Even the moon can't find you here
dense, as this dream forest is,
nor stars nor mapping fireflies nor
the phosphorous reachings of old logs.

You have gone under blankets of green sleep.
Clouds cover you.
The weathers pass you by.

You are not lost, not yet, not yet
or not unfindable, or lost
but only from our sight.
Another house
has called for you, a parent,
a wild home.

LES PÊCHEURS D'EAU

(opening image mistranslated from Anne Hébert)

The fishers of water
who sit on the pale trestles of the moon
and dangle their feet in the passing night
are pulling the ocean with their hooks
as if they thought
they turned the moon's slow partner,
earth, in its majestic do-si-do.
Perhaps they do.

Ambitious they are, each evening to let down
their nets and drag their lantern through the tides.
For centuries they've caught our music,
poets, moths, flies, frogs, dogs, cats, and lunatics.
Some years an iceberg, snagged, overturns.
So little's left, they have been fishing for so long!
Whatever they catch, they do, at least,
they do throw it all back again:
but hooked, unhooked, now maimed.

MOON SONGS

A flat tone skips on water:
rises two times.
The tap tap of the little waves,
a dancer's steps.

Moon
gathers the ripples
with its crab hands.

*

Over the prairie the night's black swan
brushes the sibilant grasses, feathers the lakes.
Mist rises toward its wing tips, thins:
invisible homage the waning moon
evaporates.

*

Where pearled reflections wash
their feet, geese rest.
Grey travellers, disciples of the dawn,
they see the earth diminish and return
beneath them in its seasons, and they mourn
death as we do, widows, widowers.

The moon
ferments and rises over them
like a white yeast.

BROMELIAD

Just as some plants live in air,
dependant from the phone lines or old stumps,
so I, unrooted, transient, align myself along a road,
a yard, or a city block.

I have no place. The wind
might move me anywhere. Though every place
is different, imbued with small disasters of its own.

I have been here for quite some time.
Almost at home, a student of the new,
the strange, the alien.

Each morning seems more lonely than the last.
The stars have faded away like dreams.
Even the seasons, familiar once,
have changed, have changed.

But have *I* changed? How shall I live?
Perhaps it only matters that I do.

PALM

The roads, the winds, not roaring, and the sky
unpricked by commerce, shadows, birds,
the sheeted yard distilled in sleep:
it seems a sort of happiness —
nothing that must, or easily,
wants to be done —

so, on the far shelves of our dreams
wait mistily
the dreads we need not look at now —
To watch the pale sky turn to cream
seems good enough: a calm
that like an empty hand held out
seems warm, seems almost welcoming,
signing the centre of hard days
with its still palm.

WHAT'S LEFT

Prayer answers I was not asking for,
or meditation when my mind
hovers between the bird song of the ear
and the loud thrumming furnace —

then floats, perhaps
above a white, imagined choir
or a blue-veined aerial nothingness
that flaps in a thin vacancy
I had no hand in.

The earth wells up around me,
warm, and rich, and dangerous.
An answer to what sort of prayer?
A thumb of yellow fungi or a bone
like coral on the moss?
Or some deep diver of the soul
who hooks the red thread's
minotaur, as frisky as a virus,
macro, live.

I remember those family picnics
when I was seven, or twelve:
the hot dogs as they never were,
mosquitoes so bland! So here,
not quite at the tail end of all things
but on the hinge,

the various knots
rust and unravel. How beautiful
the chair beneath the lamp, the rug,
the unimported yard trees or the shine
of afternoon on a scratched bench!

And if I miss
my friend, my lover, what I miss
is real, fills up the afternoon
with a strong sweetness. Nothingness
is nothing to write home about.
You were.

SERENITY

Serenity like a selfish dream
floats up and seems to coat my mind
with a slick sensuous retard.
"All's well," the inner prompter tolls.
Well, no.

But here
with the green grasses springing up,
Debussy's "Syrinx," birds
(though my ears are dull,
something inhabits the shaking trees) —

Beside me in the living room
no wilderness, no you, no bread,
but a cheap merlot and a tabby cat
that brews like a kettle on my knee,
things could be worse.

Peace settles on my shoulders like fine dust;
irrelevant, it answers to no prayer,
and coats the lucky, not the just.
We fortunates the storms passed by
can't boast.

PANSY

Gentle, the folding inward of the day,
as if the leaves, now yellowing,
fall toward a sleep,
their letting go, and, one by one,
some loose their knotted fingers.

If the wind
might stir the clouds above us, here, below,
nothing is almost trembling,
the nearly nothing, the dreaminess
of summers lost, forgotten, or ignored.

One stalwart pansy gleams
like a last thought "upon the stairs,"
anachronous, perhaps,
or rather, as protest.

Not everything
goes willingly.
Accept? Refuse? The dignity's
the same.

A late light simmers
in the trees. Tonight,
no frost.

ACKNOWLEDGEMENTS

I wish to thank the editors of the following magazines in which these poems first appeared:

The Antigonish Review: "Noise," "Palm," "The Ghost." *ARC*: "Les Pêcheurs d'Eau." *Descant*: "In a Glass Darkly." *fairsfair.com*: "Push," "She Keeps Writing the Same Poem." *The Fiddlehead*: "The Hill Cemetery at St. Martin's," "Past Midnight, Avignon," "Dali's 'Santiago,'" *The New Quarterly*: "The Sea Beyond the Church," "An Old Machine," "Window of Leaves," "Moon Songs." *Prairie Fire*: "The Confluence," "Temporarily Lost." *Prairie Journal*: "The Steeple," "Happiness: It Had Been Here," "Monkey," "Crows' Bivouac." *Rhubarb*: "Sleep Dear Child," "'I would have told you.'"

"In a Glass Darkly," "How Long?," "Her Story," "Stuff," "I Have Forgotten Your Name," "I Wish the Snow Would Come Down," and "What's Left" are reprinted from *The Book of Widows* (2010), a fine print edition with wood engravings by George A. Walker, published by Frog Hollow Press in two limited-edition bindings, seventy paperbound and thirty hardcover. My thanks to Shane Neilson and Caryl Peters.

"Old Parent," "The Tenant," and "Stone Dusk" appeared in the bilingual anthology, *Bridges Over the Saint John River/Los Puentes del Rio San Juan* (Broken Jaw Press, 2011). My thanks to Nela Rio and Joe Blades.

"The Confluence" appeared in *The Best Canadian Poetry 2009* (A. F. Moritz, editor; Tightrope Books, 2009).

Thanks also to the editor of the present collection, Robyn Sarah, for her good advice, encouragement and labour, and to the musician and composer Brenda Muller for her helpfulness and perception.

ABOUT M. TRAVIS LANE

As a child, an "army brat," Millicent Travis Lane travelled almost yearly, and had no hometown. Educated at Vassar and Cornell, she came with her family to Fredericton in 1960, where they became Canadian citizens. She is Honorary Research Associate with the English department at the University of New Brunswick, a member of Voice of Women for Peace and the Raging Grannies, and has been writing reviews for *The Fiddlehead* for half a century. Recognized as one of Atlantic Canada's most important poets, M. Travis Lane has received numerous awards for her poetry, including the Alden Nowlan Award for excellence in the English language literary arts, the Atlantic Poetry Prize, the Bliss Carman Award, and the Pat Lowther Memorial Award. *Ash Steps* is her fourteenth poetry title.